William Neill was born in Ayrshire, Scotland, in 1922. He was educated at Ayr Academy and later at Edinburgh University, where he studied Celtic languages and English as a mature student. He taught for some years in Galloway, where he now lives. In 1969 he was the Bard of the National Gaelic Mod in Aviemore. While at university he won the Sloane Prize and the Grierson Prize for poetry. He has had collections of verse published in Scotland's three tongues: Gaelic, Scots and English. His work appears frequently in magazines and has featured in radio and television broadcasts. He has read his work in various locations in Scotland, Ireland, Italy and Germany. His collection *Wild Places* (Luath Press, 1985) won a Scottish Arts Council Book Award.

Other poetry collections by William Neill:

Scotland's Castle (Reprographia, Edinburgh, 1970)
Poems (Akros, Penwortham, 1970)
Four Points of a Saltire, with Sorley MacLean, Stuart MacGregor and George Campbell Hay (Reprographia, Edinburgh, 1970)
Despatches Home (Reprographia, Edinburgh, 1972)
Galloway Landscape (Urr Publications, Castle Douglas, 1981)
Cnú a Mogaill (Celtic Department, Glasgow University, Glasgow, 1983)
Wild Places (Luath Press, Barr, Ayrshire, 1985)
Blossom, Berry, Fall (Fleet Intec, Gatehouse-of-Fleet, 1986)
Making Tracks (Gordon Wright, Edinburgh, 1988)

STRAIGHT LINES

WILLIAM NEILL

THE
BLACKSTAFF PRESS
BELFAST

Some of these poems have appeared in the following:
Agenda, Cencrastus, Chapman, Envoi, New Writing Scotland, Orbis, Outposts, Poetry Wales, Scot Free, Scots Magazine, Scotsman, Spectrum.

First published in 1992 by
The Blackstaff Press Limited
3 Galway Park, Dundonald, Belfast BT16 0AN, Northern Ireland
with the assistance of
The Arts Council of Northern Ireland

Typeset by Textflow Services Limited

Printed by The Guernsey Press Company Limited

British Library Cataloguing in Publication Data

Neill, William
Straight lines.
I. Title
821.914
ISBN 0-85640-475-6

for Dodo

CONTENTS

STONE CIRCLE

All kinds of reasons given
for these stone circles;
the summer adder and the shrieking gull
know them as well as man.

Megaliths not worn down
by long millennia.
How shall we know
what prompting set this granite firmly here?

What on this desert moor called sweating men
to numinous idea and the fulfilment?
Sun sets, sun rises over menhir:
gives to their ancient smoothness
the glint of gold or blood.

SUNSET TOUCH

The last day of the year —
a red and amber sunset.

Standing on the knowe above calm water,
the quiet grazing beasts
watch as I watch the swans
breaking the reflections of bare trees,
shadow of hill and cloud.

The burden of old memories, new fears,
for one clear moment
is lifted from the heart.

NAMES

There is no way to compass mystery
in all the words of specious erudition
scrabbling to find its own rock-hard position
on the cliff-face of black uncertainty.
You can't stand firm on any -ology;
this thing won't wear the fetters of tradition,
though something's there beyond the range of vision
that won't be bounded by doxology.

Choose what to call it: Nothing, He, She, That,
the Good, the Ground of Being, Deep Within.
Underneath all there's surely a Foundation.

But not a hook to hang a shovel-hat
that, magic, makes the seen of the unseen.
Five senses cannot balance the equation.

TRESPASS

A new man, strange and richer, comes and puts
his mark across the gate of our old lane:
bald PRIVATE PROPERTY; the ancient wood
that once we all enjoyed is closed again.

Anger: then memory of the old man, dead.
Now, minding on his generous grace, I lie
awake upon this windy winter morning,
seeing his shared flowers in the mind's eye.

ETHICAL PROBLEM

'Twas a Friday night when they set sail
and they were not far from the land,
when the submarine turned up her tail
and stuck her nose in the sand.

'Don't panic me lads,' cried Skipper Pete,
'for we'll soon be out of here,
with our snorkels and our flipper feet
and our patent escaping gear.'

Then he called to Joe, the bosun's mate –
'You're the oldest man in the crew,
and you haven't looked any too good of late
and besides – you're a grandad too.'

'Thanks, Cap'n Pete,' said the bosun's mate,
that matlow as plump as pork.
'A man o' my trim and tonnage weight
should bob to the top like cork.'

Weep, shipmates, for that fatal day
the skipper chose Sailor Joe,
for he jammed the hatch like a bung of clay
and would neither come nor go.

'Well, that's a rum 'un,' the skipper said,
'and fairly tries my wits;
we'd better break a cutlass out
and carve him into bits.

'On the other hand, it's hardly fair
– although I'm tempted sore –
to chop up a chap with not much hair
and grandsons by the score.'

So there they sit in the deep blue sea
all along of Davy Jones,
trapped by the skipper's morality
and their shipmate's sixteen stones.

HIGH OR LOWLY

The rich man's castle and the poor man's gate
are not a feature of the hymn book now,
deleted by a recent churchly row
whose outcome was that, though much sung of late,
such sentiments, on modern feelings, grate.
Egalitarian ways had shown us how
Dives and Lazarus in this vale below
could both be flatly levelled by the State.

Though now the duke has opened up the Hall
to let the plebs in for a pound a head,
if you ask me, despite his blue-blood whinge,
he doesn't do too badly after all:
wine cellar, game preserve, four-poster bed.
My poor man's gate rots on its single hinge.

GILLESPIE'S WOOD

Bright Monday and I walking
from the black croft to the rushy glen,
under the shade of trees by the riverside,
grass growing freshly in the wood-clearings,
calm in the heavens and on the river-pool,
everything under the quiet of early spring,
and my eye often on each hill crowned
with a gleam of late winter snow.

The white swan and his faithful lover
swim stately by on the smooth mirror,
the snowdrop spread on every bank
and the daffodil coming to bloom.
A gentle man is Gillespie,
who will kill no creature for sport;
each bird and beast with the way of its kind
and I one with all creation.

Standing at peace among these trees,
oak and birch, yew and beech,
that started many a year before me
and grew free from bite of saw or axe;
my hope – they wave loftily
their noble branches in the clear sky
many a long year over the head of Gillespie,
who saved the crown of the forest for us.

RESPITE

No conversation here but the wind's voice,
the rustle of trees, bird song and secret calls
in dark or moonlight. Frost crisp over grass,
rain on the cheek. After the rumbling city
this peace assails the ear.

Time here for sundry old philosophies
that hang from boughs or whisper among leaves.

Here is the land lost to the high concrete,
from tabled gatherings where important sounds
are rustled papers, tappings, clinking metals.

Here we examine the thought
that the confines of flesh hold all.

Or that the woods and water are one with the beholder.

TWO BLACK FINGERS

Our motor-culture vies with conservation:
not only human carnage, beasts as well
are smashed and flattened in our speeding hell,
as business travellers roar towards consummation,
too great to brake for those of lesser station.
Death of the noble pheasant seems a waste,
crushed to a bloody bone-and-feather paste
before the annual shotgun termination.

The other day I passed a slaughtered crow.
Undone at last by his too-urgent greed,
he lay with funeral plumage all unfurled
and mocked from this last nest the ancient foe.
Since wingless we remain for all our speed,
two feathers raised, like fingers, to the world.

SPRING FROST

The spring has nearly gone
yet there is still
a drift upon the hill,
a frost on the green lawn.
Silent, I gaze and gaze
across the gleam of gold,
happy near-summer's blazon
on this unseemly cold
that halts our growing season,
till joy in the morning is brought
to sudden, sadder thought.

THE WINDOWS

Confined to the grim tower of the five windows
fixed in the stones, forcing the eyes one way,
the prisoner sees a sky that never shows
a travelling sun to light his cruel day.

Always a mist rolls over the grey land,
telling the captive – this is all there is:
the same dull bleakness, always, on every hand
the eye is caged in lasting wilderness.

He cannot tell what lies behind the tower;
futile behind these doors to speculate.
A garden bright with everlasting flowers?
A stark ravine beyond the castle gate?

To be freed at last only when heaven's dark
and the step falters, voice dies on the wind?
The captive blesses his captor, into the mirk
fixes his gaze, to dreaming landscapes blind.

HOUYHNHNMS AREN'T REAL HORSES

The good Dean Swift said he preferred the horse
to 'odious little vermin' – you and me.
I find I don't entirely agree;
in many ways the quadruped is worse.
I've had first-hand experience, of course,
which tends to make the disenchanted see
how downright nasty nags can often be.
Their actions can provoke a hasty curse.

When they've been idly snoozing in a stall,
waiting for cereal hand-outs, in you come;
they bite you fiercely on the upper arm.
Or else they give a playful sideways roll,
against the traverse crush your chest and tum,
which detracts somewhat from that equine charm.

HOMEBOUND

The night before you went you told me how
by dint of Latin learning and much Greek
you dodged the barn and byre and left the plough
for joy of books in learning's ancient seat.

How as a schoolboy, reading on the bus,
you hoped the evening milking would be over;
how your two sisters would complain and fuss
at having extra dairying to cover.

Now, craft destroyed, you lie beside the bones
of those old Greeks and Romans, long since drowned
beneath that middle sea. Paroxytones,
georgics, anacreontics robbed of sound.

DETERMINISM

Am I a crude computer made of meat?
It seems unlikely on this busy street
where men steer cars to right or left at will
(except when a red light bids them be still).

Love is not love. Despite the poet's art
of fostering passion in the tender heart,
is this mere essence of a sexual chemistry
of atoms passing between thee and me?

If Good Intent and High Romance are dead,
thinking's electron-shuffling in the head,
not from the Muse my random verses flow
but along iron rails forged long ago.

SINGING

It was seldom calm; most nights the usual wind
from Ireland across the machair, but no rain.
I walked in those light nights to the halfway inn
to drink myself singing. English words faded
as the night wore on. A body could believe
the song would never die in spite of all.

Homeward in that late twilight; abbey walls
rose to the skyline on the further island.
Surely their songs were holier far than ours,
bawled out in drink in that rough hostelry?

But lonely there upon the morning shore,
knowing that in those taproom choruses
there was a yearning deep as sanctity.

BENEATH ALL

Under these singing birds,
oak, ash and pine,
these peaceful swans that sail,
is that for which all words,
each man-made sign,
shall for all striving fail.

Layer upon layer lies.
All human pride,
and deepest reason fails
beneath these mysteries
that move and change and glide
beneath seen hills, seen dales.

DAUBER'S DEATH

Coming from the pub, we saw the sky alight
down by the alder wood: Burne-Tumber's place,
that even the tramps considered a disgrace.
The flames climbed high and crackled in the night,
but of His Painting Craziness, no sight.
So fierce the fire we never found a trace
of flesh or bone or button or bootlace;
with easel, paint and brush cremated quite.

Seeing his life's work burning, couldn't stay.
Into the flames with neither pail nor hose
he dashed to rescue just one daub too many.

He stacked the others fifty yards away.
Mad as a hare to risk his neck for *those*.
Oddly enough, they fetched a pretty penny.

KING LOURIE

The king's hair is long
for his barber is slain,
he calls me to comb out
and sleek his great mane.

Tall tree of the Harpstrings,
now answer me fair,
why does he slay barbers
who trim his long hair?

*His crown is of gold
and his sceptre of pearls,
but the ears of a donkey
are hid by his curls.*

What then shall I do
when I barber his head?

*Make sure you are shriven
for soon you'll be dead.*

FAIRY TALES

One at a time you throw them all away:
Red Girl and Silly Jack, Wolf and Wise Crow.
They held a kind of wonder in their day,
but vision narrows, so they have to go.

Make room for stories of a tighter kind:
constructed shapes and lines that never meet
for ever and ever. In the end the mind
discovers none of these is quite complete.

Gold turned to dross. We look again at tales
heard in far childhood. Wolf and crow come back,
call in the night. The magic galley sails
on inner seas, upon another tack.

STORM AWAKENING

The wind rattles the slates, in the deep night
elements chip at the fabric of the walls;
wake, wake to the gale's threat that fills the blackness.

All life is caught within a terrifying instant;
brackets containing a known quantity
approaching the limit of the infinitely small.
Outside the brackets, the unsolved unknowns
stretch to eternity. There is no order,
no seeming purpose in existence
within this monstrous and unanswering wilderness.

Useless to kick stones in the mind and say – this is reality.
Nor does truth lie in vanishing differentials
or the imagined ends of aleph-null.
In the country of the blind, who knows the spectrum?

Now there is no escape in sleep from fear.
Count to infinity, the square roots under ten,
to be or not to be, remembered litanies.
Old murmured intercessions, half believed
until the mind clears to an empty screen.

HOUSE BY THE WATER

Long since I was a guest in that lone house.
Tall windows staring across the water
at the white church tower beyond the green knowes
where wildfowl whirr upwards and geese clatter.

The late sun drapes the walls with gold and red,
the water slips to the sea and mocks my pity
for the man fled, the woman silent and sad,
for the children gone, claimed by a far city.

BUREAUCRAT

No wonder you're sealed off against attack
by stout plate glass: only the merest slot
allows communication; you are not
one of us plebs queuing for ten yards back.
Your job is guaranteed against the sack
for life, unless you're actually caught
with fingers in the till. I'm sure it's thought
this mile-long queue makes rebel instincts slack.

You are the buffer between Them and Us.
Your pachydermal front keeps Them from view
behind a wall of bumf that's ten feet thick.

We wait because we hate to make a fuss.
Some day we sheep will find someone like you
inside hell's turnstile, working for Old Nick.

ELEMENTS

Now that the City's banished the old notions,
knocked down the stones of every holy shrine,
phlogiston's vanished with the older potions,
new Nothingness is given the magic sign.
Remove all space, you make a point so fine
the schoolmen's certainties are seen for chance,
their angels left no pin whereon to dance.

Yet woods seem timeless, where beneath the foot
earth moves and speaks to every sharpened sense.
Soil holds old skull and bone and growing root;
the time-crushed rocks and inching filament
nurse all that comes to living lineament:
staple of blessed saint and blooded claws,
the sacrificial knife, the shrine that draws.

Though wind no longer wanders as of old
nor holds the pneuma, we are not confused
because the City says the spirit's cold,
and colder reason in the soul infused;
tells us old Zeus and Mumbo Jumbo, used
as ancient superstition's kittle-cattle,
now bolster modern sacerdotal rattle.

The smothering blanket of the distant City
has made the flame of passion duly pass;
the sun cools down, they say, and that's a pity.
Yet still there's heat beneath the rotting grass;

down in the forest those old tales may last;
when City stone cracks with synthetic frost
the fire that warmed the cave may warm the most.

Still the deep waters shimmer to the sight
where life's first jelly chanced, they say, unmade;
the stream that flows between the dark and light
still can't be crossed by mortal flesh or shade,
but still the subtle essence that first played
across the waters gleams before the eye,
when soul seeks what the City thinks a lie.

Feet press again the City-banished earth;
breast feeds upon the air; the spirit lives
within the ancient wind that gave it birth,
a flame to life the lasting fire still gives.
In these deep woods the hidden wonder moves;
when eyes are opened and the blood stream sings,
man finds new names for older, wiser things.

LOCKERBIE

Dawn comes up and the mist rises from the hill,
the people move again on the wounded streets.

The little town, after the day's concerns,
settling to leisure and the quiet time,
became in darkness a bull's-eye for blind hate.
Whose the skilled fingers, grown from a child's,
that primed a clever fuse to slaughter innocence?

Still, to the guiltless, death comes in the night
in ways all unforeseen. The well-wisher
burns in the fire of opinionated malice;
the humble roof is crushed
beneath the weight of the mind's mad tyranny.

They are mingled now in death, the joyous hearts
that were bound homewards in a festal time,
a unity with those who walked these streets.

And evil finds no yield in the clear souls
of those who yet remain; what man calls grace
triumphs at last over the setters of snares.

As dawn comes up and the mist fades on the hill.

DESIRING THIS MAN'S ART . . .

In a bleak cabin beside salty flats
Burne-Tumber spent his last precarious days,
oblivious to either wealth or praise,
sharing his frugal fare with gulls and cats.
He would not paint rich dames in flowered hats
nor seek to catch their lordships' haughty gaze.
No story-pictures of the cheerful ways
of vinous cardinals in fireside chats.

Now fortunes pass to buy his coloured boards:
ten thousand for a landscape would be cheap.
His guarded paintings grace the gallery wall.

The summer painters come down here in hordes,
hoping to rouse Burne-Tumber's ghost from sleep.
Alas, he doesn't speak to them at all.

COAST ROAD

Once, said my father, scarce a body came
along this road. Sometimes a pony and trap
would meet another and the drivers swap
a word between the marketplace and home.

Now nose to tail along the crowded shore,
they weave and dodge and risk their necks to pass
between the hillside and the marram grass.
No sound but blasting horn and engine roar.

Dad's time was slow: now you can fairly fly
past the whole rocky coastline in a day,
eyes on the road, no longer need to stay
and idle by the verge with passers-by.

NEIL MACVURICH'S LOST POEMS

After the generations passed,
his seed, lowered from bards to tailors,
found the old vellum lying in a chest.

History robbed them of learning
in their own ancient tongue.
No harm it seemed to them
to cut up hide in tapes to measure cloth.

Be sparing of your sneers.
They could not read.
Blame those who read
and smother poets with a boor's indifference.

LISTEN, MUSE

Please, let another poem come tomorrow,
next week and the week after yet another,
from the old sacred word-hoard. Let me borrow
true coin till geriatric mists so smother
the sinking brain that I no longer care
whether the lines are end-stopped, whether rhyme.
To that brief dimness that dissolves despair
in the slow rooms of second-childhood time,
I will surrender. But until that day
let me join word to word in brightest hope
that some new singing bird will soar for me
and I will catch its clear fresh climbing note.
If the mind fails, so that all past loves die,
let one fine sonnet breathe a farewell sigh.

FLY FISHING

Tonight, from fly and rise, concentric rings
move on the loch across a millpond calm;
they stir the mind to other patterned things,
in other depths that sain the soul from harm.

At last the floating circles tire the eyes,
lose line in shadow as the hour grows late.
In a blank stillness let the fisher wait
above the bank where wisdom's salmon lies.

RED

Ribs of trees on the ridge,
bare hawthorn on the breast of a red sun
sinking behind hills in the tight grip of December.

A sheep long dead,
bones picked bare on the moor,
and the red glow lighting white ribs.

For all the chill of winter,
under my own ribs the red blood still runs.
I look through bones and tree at the crimson west,
clasping us all into the one redness.

FOREWARNING

'No more than a mere competent versifier,'
they say of those who use such things as rhymes
in our line-chopping and informal times.
I don't let insult cloud my mind with ire,
remembering that great Byron did not tire
of making matching noises end his lines
long before Ogden Nash. These were the signs
that once gave entry to the bardic choir.

Dactyl and trochee have gone out of fashion,
but that's the kind of trick I was brought up on.
They think it mere nostalgia and back-harking.

Old-fashioned schoolmasters taught me a passion
for formal verses. I don't care a button
that mine are often sonnets . . . and Petrarchan.

PRAGMATIST

Doctor Al Embick has improved his sight,
sees fairyland with electronic eye,
knows that mere six-six vision's not quite right,
and shares the compound vision of the fly.

The universe is made of Nothingness,
with empty spaces layered in its strands.
Good as a concept is quite meaningless,
evil a matter of imperfect glands.

Knowledge is all; let bare hypothesis
bend to the disciplined experiment;
the truth is not as laymen think it is.
Space is not infinite or bound, but bent.

You can't see heaven through a telescope,
only the Pleiades. Those quarks and such
deny the comfort of the caveman's hope:
steeplehouse-keepers cannot tell you much.

H. Bosch is bosh. Those horns and hooves and tails
look very well in medieval paint.
Empirical investigation fails
to register the halo of the saint.

HIGH-LEVEL STUFF

Necrotic PLC have built a plant
to manufacture Ersatz Coprofate.
Public Inquiries first, some seven or eight,
whose experts smiled at all our clueless cant
against what They Who Know Much Better want.
It opened up slap on the planning date,
a warning death's-head high up on the gate.
Now we've developed an asthmatic pant.

The new calves have three legs, the babes, one eye;
our gums are bleeding and our tongues turn blue.
Investigators can't apportion blame.

The smoke may smell, they say, but we won't *die*:
MPs they've sponsored, retained lawyers, too.
You'll pay the costs, if you contest the claim.

SO FAIR A FANCY

What would you say if I should tell you all
I saw upon the hill the other night:
an angel sitting on a dry-stone wall,
his pinions gleaming in a mystic light?

A sight that poor Tom Hardy never saw,
but wished he had; the Immanence of Will
smacks of a granite Scientific Law,
not like my angel sitting on a hill.

If I should swear it on my mother's grave
you'd hesitate to say I was a liar,
but send for a psychiatrist to save
my head from harm, if not my soul from fire.

Ah well, I didn't see one, any more
than Tommy Hardy saw at Christmas time
the oxen kneeling on the stable floor
and put his longing in a bonny rhyme.

I thought it worth my while to tell a lie
that made your life less boring. My romance
sprang from the mood that made Tom Hardy sigh;
hope against hope we hadn't lost the chance.

MOOR

Here on this open land there is no belief
in the formulations of men.

Behind this beauty the flying seeds of infinity
will suffer no set creed.

The mind that frames no liturgy
can find no altar for old sacrifice.

THROWBACK

From their firm teachings he had been shot back
into his own historical time warp,
strummed on an old guitar with a long crack,
thinking on long-lost days of the strung harp.

He climbed again to the stone-circled hill,
in the noon sun or under the moon's travel,
to hear old riddles from the buried skull,
words that the newer books could not unravel.

Seeking a time before the good men came;
to break the fiddle's belly, snap the pipe,
though death or madness took them just the same,
as in the dancing days when fields were ripe.

PEEL TOWER

In the river's eye,
breached walls of a square keep,
a monument to tyranny
crushed by a new oppression.

Proof against blades
battered to death by shot.
The island shore a slovenly mosaic,
the adamantine tesserae
scorched by a dragon's breath.

A tumbled temple of Mars
founded on fear and greed,
the vulture penates
fled to a surer stronghold.

The leaves are not yet fallen; changing now,
they pay their tribute gold to autumn's green.
The long glass of the loch lies calm between
the stretching moorland and the distant view,
where hillsides fade through brown to misty blue.
To save a fall to winter's dearth, unseen,
how often this fair countryside has been
tried upon canvas with a painter's hue.

Showing in galleries a mere magic place,
a nowhere-country of the artist's mind,
a coloured plane sought by an inner yearning.

Yet real enough today September's grace,
the quiet time that helps the soul to find
a fleeting joy may shine in the year's turning.

VEIL

As if it had not been,
the grey mists cover
all we have ever seen
of life and lover.
Where we have yet to be
the dark clouds hover,
hiding what we shall see
before all's over.

WINDFALLS

My ladder's not so much gone as my legs,
so I can't reach the topmost apples now.
Barred from the purchase of rich dates and figs,
I must make all the best of windfalls do.

Yet they're as sweet, for all their marks and flaws,
as any that I had of fruit before.
The passing years have compensating laws:
when we lose much, we prize the little more.

HOME THOUGHTS IN THE PIAZZA

We were remote and running on scythed wheels,
when these were polished, regular, urbane,
between the *altopiano* and the plain
where Dante's compeers rigged their daggered schemes.

Sweet-sounding strings, under an evening sky
smooth as shot silk above the colonnade.
Where mercenaries marched and Caesar played,
we sit and sip within a warm wind's sigh.

On our wet moorland, by their last frontier,
brown water rages white through scattered stone;
this, our first sculpture, carved by time alone,
stubbornly in our vision even here.

TIMEPIECE

Now the celestial watchmaker is bored
with planetoid escapements: those verge rings
of calculated spheres, sidereal swings
of stars upon the end of Kepler's cord.
We grow uncertain that the heavenly horde
points our endeavours towards much better things;
return to a hopeless version: voyagings
of stones whose spheral tune will not be heard.

Yet with no lens to aid the naked eye,
the stars still hold their wonder in the deep
unplumbed abyss of pure infinity.

To simpler thought the constellations lie,
secure within an older plan, and keep
their many-jewelled bearings running free.

BANK HOLIDAY

Cars arrive, boats in tow. Holiday homes
bought by free enterprise and lawyers' fees
are filled again with willing refugees.
An optimistic band of anglers comes
to line the bank where our dark water runs.
The city comes to seek a fleeting ease
under wild heavens, within sight of trees,
recall imagined days of childhood suns.

The strait, stiff pews are full in the small church —
a sop to a remembered holiness.
Christmas and Easter promise a good crowd,
engaged upon its own peculiar search
for an old ghost to rise again and bless,
for life to grow from an abandoned shroud.

MULL FERRY

O fair young Mairead, love has wounded me,
O fair young lass with eyes as dark as sloes . . .

We should have booked much earlier:
the car deck's absolutely packed.

The silver salmon I would take for you,
rich venison upon the hills of Mull . . .

The scenery's marvellous, those hills and things.
But the people! A depressing lot.

Eyes clear as dewdrops hanging from the branch,
so blue and still in the early morn . . .

The important things, of course,
all run by people like ourselves.

O fair young Mairead, were I only there
in the high mountains of Mull with you . . .

CONSIDER THE LILIES

Down by the loch, geese
laugh at the weather,
happy and handsome
in their fine feather.

Midshipman crawler,
climbing a nettle,
grows to an admiral
rigged in rare fettle.

Goats on the mountain
stand on a pebble,
ruminate calmly
on their high level.

Ragged and starving
in that dark city,
live other creatures
in need of pity.

LOW FLYERS

Above the ridge-tile and the sleeping slate
ten tons of metal boom. Jove's thunder seems
mere myth indeed beside this bursting weight
of warlike clamour riding on man-made flames.

Yet in this quiet place above green lawns
the sky finds room for other wings. We hear
the swishing pinions of grey morning swans
move on the misted stillness of the air.

CONVENTICLE

On these long, drizzling moors the faithful met:
the moss-hag minister and stubborn saint,
fearless of wounds and a far king's complaint,
being in their holy righteousness well set.
Some echo of their sermons bides here yet
among bare heather under a dour sky.
We, in agnostic armour, merely sigh
for their old causes; we deny the debt.

Admire these martyrs of unyielding mind
for a grim courage. Questioning its root,
our minds contest the certainties they claimed.

In this bleak loneliness, in this cold wind,
they died in trust. We, drowning under doubt,
circled by their stone monuments, are shamed.

BEANSTALK

Jacko swaps a cow for beans,
seems to profit from the sale:
quite by accident he gains
fame and fortune. Likely tale.

High as Jack may mount the stalk,
life is harder than the fable.
Golden goose and singing harp
stay upon the giant's table.

REJECTION

A child, he wandered long on that wild shore,
talking with fishermen in their old tongue,
sharing their voyages. His world was young
and happiness would last for evermore.

But other voyages he made in school,
past ancient islands with the cunning Greek,
losing the older way for learning's sake,
leaving the common for a tighter rule.

Then, filled with peace, assaulted much by war,
tried to return to quieter ways again,
seeking once more those brave and simple men
unchanged in memory, kindly as before.

In near-forgotten daily phrases spoke
the childhood words, but their replies were cold,
seeing a learned man should make so bold
as think they lacked the language of the book.

Nor would they let him walk the streaming deck
that was delight so many years ago.
He tried, in yearning solitude, to go,
sharing their toil upon the sea's broad back.

They would not have it: now no more their kind.
Much learning and much time had soiled his blood.
Saddened at last, turned by their sullen mood,
he sought again the learned city's mind.

Neither the old tongue nor the learned speech
pleased their cold pedants. After long away
he roamed its streets to pass each lonely day
till crazy death put words beyond his reach.

PEACE AND PAIN

The path stretches the length of the long wood:
only myself walking. Quiet swans sail,
rippling their wakes upon an opaque pool
under a still sky. Once more tall trees are clad
in a green summer glory. Now abed,
the creatures of the night are hidden, till
a dying sun moves them to wake and prowl.
Peace comes to me and nagging thought is dead.

Yet easement goes when thought returns again
in the small hours when memory murders sleep
and cries break through the silence of the night.

A sharp and fearful scream of sudden pain
from forest darkness. Now the bright day's hope
ebbs in the thought of wild pursuit and flight.

RIVER

Men once gave a god's name to this river
that shrank to summer pools where secret fish
lay silently until a wriggling rush
gave that divinity their flash of silver.
Then spate and foaming crags where salmon covered
the roaring cataracts in a writhing dash
and fell again until a desperate lash
failed them or bore their strength in triumph over.

But that was then. Now in the sluggish deeps
is sunless darkness where no fishes glide
above a river bottom foully dressed
with different clay where nothing swims nor sleeps,
the otters long fled from the waterside.
The god is as forgotten as the rest.

NURSERY RHYME

'I'm sad,' said the Giant
in his high tower,
'for the sins I committed
in an evil hour.

'I flattened their houses
under my feet,
and stole their cattle
for my daily meat.

'Lifted their roofs off
with fee-fi-fo-fummery,
robbed all their larders
to make me a flummery.'

Then sadly he belched,
gave his belly a rub,
wiped off a tear
as he lifted his club.

'I'll be kinder,' said he,
'I will watch what I do,
take care where I step,
flatten only a few.

'But a man has to eat,
with a stomach like mine.
My deeds must be bad,
though my feelings are fine.'

FAMINE AND PLENTY

These lived full-bellied in the starving-time
under that grand roof without seeming care,
thinking the hunger none of their affair;
sat with a jaded appetite to dine,
drowning concern under a stronger wine.
Did they, with eyes turned to the girding wall
that kept at bay the starving beggar's call,
think their plush sanctuary God's design
for men too weak to beat ploughshares to swords,
the milkless women feeding babes on roots
whose poison burned their bowels in slow death,
while these ruled on, bolstered with legal words?
Did they think earth was theirs, and all its fruits,
untainted by the stink of famine's breath?

WINTER SOLSTICE

The north wind whispers to the iron frost.
Bare hawthorn trees upon the long hill ridge
reach out black arms towards the scarlet west,
where our last sun died under that bleak edge.

Knowing or not, let all the yule fires burn.
If fear or joy has made our voices rough,
from this day's embers new suns will return
to high meridian if we sing enough.

THE GENIE

For long years prisoned by a tyrant cork
in a foul bottle, he could not escape,
so lay inert in his abandoned hope
or shouted in the all-enclosing dark.

Until set free at last by a strange hand
to grow in power and sail on the light air,
singing to those who once would never hear
his shouts of rage, his black and drowned command.

IN A CATHEDRAL

No easy task, under these vaulted ceilings,
faith-bearing candles, jewel-gleaming panes,
to hold with firmness to more modern feelings.
Faced with old stones, our cynicism wanes.
Or, with thought vanquished under a clear night,
all remains true until intruding thought
brings speculation in to mist the heavens' light,
as preachings bring the numen's case to nought.
Well, close your eyes and ears and bar out all
those seepings that disturb the waking mind
and in sweet silence seek another call.
Who's to be blamed for faith, or lack of it?
In quietness alone the soul is lit.

GROWING OLD

It isn't your own ageing that is worst,
but well-beloved faces growing older,
the wrinkles on the skin that was at first
so smooth and lovely. Later love's no colder
than sex is when the blood cools. The best love
stays and grows stronger when the aching heart
knows that the sweet days pass and lovers move
inexorably on, and soon must part.

GREENWOOD

Peace lives deep in the wood throughout the seasons –
winter of bare tree, summer of heavy leaf,
sweet spring of bud, glory of golden fall –
no sound but the calling bird and the wind's sigh,
no motion but swaying branch and rustling leaf.

The fool's dead eye misses the tree's mystery,
accepts no question that can give no answer.
The soul's door closes on old magic tales;
the legends that were jewels in the mind
are smothered under muddy arrogance.

Those who still wander in remaining woods
fear to be driven out and caged again
in the far city where the day's accounting
assumes the gloss of a consensual sanity.

BIBLE-CLASS TEACHER

Mr Munro,
now you must know
the truth of those questions
we posed long ago.

Dust unto dust,
everyone must;
even you under
that God's-acre crust.

But we are still here.
In faith or in fear
we seek for an answer
in Bible or beer.

Though we often recall
the musty kirk hall
where as infants we learned
of the Rise from the Fall.

If anyone's bound,
it was you, to be crowned.
Or are you mere chemicals
under the ground?

Skull-grin or bright face,
whatever the case,
in life you brought light
with a natural grace.

NO MORE, NO MORE

'No more to the river,'
said the old one,
'though it flow for ever
when I am gone.'

'No more to the long wood,'
said the old one,
'strong as ever stood
when I am gone.'

'No more to the high hill,'
said the old one,
'and the gloaming still
when I am gone.'

'But nothing's lost,'
said the old one,
'if my pale ghost
still walks thereon.'

Never attempt to curve the reader's lip
into a smile with verses They call 'light';
the critics think there's something not quite right
in lines whose tropes embrace a merry quip.
Thalia's the very least of those who sip
the fount of Hippocrene; poetic height
is measured in High Seriousness. That bright
jewel of sparkling humour don't let slip.

Be grave, if you would have your name appear
in magazines whose purpose is High Art;
fun verse is not the stuff to get you in.

Keep your wit's feather from the groundling ear.
Write about Love and Death but don't impart
a hint that Death's expression is a grin.

WILD THINGS

Last night the woods were empty of humankind;
whispering trees, the gloaming cry of birds,
the flashing speckle of a startled hind,
but no shouts, no words.

Today the hounds bell over far fields,
wild things rush out from the shotguns' rattle,
the gun dogs wait till bid at their masters' heels,
keen for the battle.

It all depends on when your folks came over –
if with King Fergus then you'll be all right . . .
the Pict admixture makes you Scottish quite,
but from the Tattie Blight you can't recover.

Even if your lot are somewhere in the middle,
between King Fergie and the British Raj,
you can't dodge flute and shamrock, sash and badge,
or play mere Scottish reels upon your fiddle.

Wear non-committal colours, say there is no God,
and preach no texts except the Left Book Club . . .
hot bigotry makes room in any pub
for Papist Atheist and Agnostic Prod.

Kentigern's salmon swallowed a gold ring
and spewed it up beside the Dear Green Place . . .
a symbol for the Scoto-Irish race
whose hammers crashed on steel like anything.

The liveried buses rove in Orange and Green . . .
splendidly neutral through the city wards;
along the river, past the silent yards,
more fitting target for sectarian spleen.

DEER

Seen between tall trunks of oak and beech,
the heads of deer, the veined leaf-ears erect
before the graceful flight, their secret reach
jolted by memory of far-smiting death.

Even from the best of marks, the writhing legs,
the misting eye, the agony from the throat;
wounds from the clashing battle-antlers of stags,
the leech of age, less instant than the shot.

Each warm live creature has its way to go
in darkness, forever parted from the herd.
Strange time denies in mercy they should know
the moment chosen by the verderer's word.

TRACKS

The polished rails lay on their sleepers here;
their leaving made another country lane.
Now wildness has reclaimed the bank again,
tracks of the line and footpath disappear.
At first, mere twigs; but steadily each year
a longer branch. Where the dead sleepers lay,
beech, sycamore will climb the sky one day,
free wings alone disturb the country air.

Hedgehog and fox travel the secret nights;
wild apples loose their treasure in the fall;
the sentry bramble claws invading feet.

After mankind returns the stolen rights,
it doesn't take the others long at all
to move along the old familiar beat.

THE SEARCH

With fond hope he came back to that old place,
warmly thinking again to find old roots,
having distantly come to a new kind of grace
in their strange music, magical words in books.

To climb into those hills from his flat plain;
to stand on summits breathing the fine air;
to make familiar each strange-sounding name,
such willing enterprise could hardly fail.

For was he not bred of their blood and mind,
driven by oppression from that native place,
his very name the mark of their own kind?
His fathers' lungs had drunk the selfsame air.

To share some essence of their stranger homes,
with their words on his lips he ventured back,
seeking to tread their unfamiliar slopes,
to set his hand upon unyielding rock.

But in the end, trapped by his own flat land,
the far horizon with no skyline hill,
woke from the dream his alien mind had planned,
mere phantoms ordered by a seeking will.

MS DICKINSON (1830–1886)

Think of bright Emily sitting quietly there
in her lone room, arrayed in virgin white,
a metaphor that fitted her aright.
High Poetry was much more her affair,
though dull male editors could hardly bear
to read her verses; their opinion quite
that knitting or embroidery was the height
of Art permissible in female care.

Needlepoint frames could not contain the writer;
other designs she had, despite those males.
Knowing posterity would well requite her,
wrapped in brown paper all her nightingales
with sure and neat instructions for a brighter
posthumous generation, rising sales.

MIDGES AT HERCULANEUM

Culex that night was vicious. Marcus Opimus
felt their sharp daggers in his scented hide,
cursed the dull lackey whose pretended fuss
bred keener edge in that bloodthirsty tribe.

Above the town the ancient mountain rumbled
as Vulcan blew his forge to glowing fire.
Marcus well knew that smithy's cry-wolf grumbles,
considered gnat-stabbings a deal more dire.

Now cased in lava, slave and Marcus lie,
armoured from stings within their sure defences;
attract the idle traveller's curious eye,
the probing insolence of camera lenses.

THE MILLMAN

October's moon over the evening yard,
rumble of wheels upon the rutted road,
breaking the earth, for all the frost was hard
under that iron load.

Steam tractor, threshing mill and caravan
come there to part their straw and chaff and grain,
the final fruiting of the peasant plan,
reward of labour's pain.

Into the firelit room the millman came,
with a hook for a hand, a face as pale as death;
the child, who saw all grown men as the same,
drew in a frightened breath.

The millman only grinned and waved his hook,
stuck down his corpse's face to the boy's head:
I'm more alive, my laddie, than I look.
It's just my hand that's dead . . .

and buried too, for it was never found
when the engine skidded on the bank and fell.
I often sit and think about that hand,
waiting in heaven or hell.

IS THAT ALL?

Is that all?
The to-ing and fro-ing,
the tickling and hurting,
the darkness, the knowing,
the oozing and spurting.
Is that all?

Is that all?
The struggling and striving,
the laughing, the crying,
the husband-and-wifing,
the living, the dying.
Is that all?

Is that all?
The head and the heart,
the soul and the mind,
the skill and the art,
the kin and the kind . . .
between cradle and grave
what more would you have?

LITERATURE PANEL

. . . it's important not to be crushed.
Philip Larkin

An invitation to this latest show . . .
certainly boosts my literary credit.
Thanks for the invitation. Nice to know
you like my latest book. (But has he read it?)

They'll all be there, the Oxbridge academics,
talking above my head about Eng. Lit.,
looking down noses at my past polemics . . .
reducing me with their High Table wit.

It's useless taking drink to bolster courage;
wine doesn't work, beer makes me want to pee . . .
when for some subtle quote I try to forage,
all memory's drowned by Scotch and G and T.

I ought to go to stop my stock from falling;
writers must live within the public eye,
to talk about the problems of their calling . . .
but when I'm asked to give my views I die.

I feel I'd like to go, and yet I know,
from such past meetings, booze will take its toll.
Dilemma's horns: to go or not to go,
remain unknown, or struck from honour's roll?

MUSICAL FORMULA

The minstrels play
their tricks upon a ladder that appears
to set for them the maker's given strain;
such airs the common airs again relay.
Two drums that echo in attendant ears
beat their dark rhythms to the darker brain.

A string vibrates,
a crafted wooden chamber subtly trembles –
is music stolen from the moving air?
What dusty word convincingly relates,
or casual thought with any truth resembles,
the deep enchantment of this strange affair?

TIME SERVER

Pity the man who waited till too late
to marshal thought, take on his proper task,
after a weakness he had blamed on fate
that made him lose true looking for the mask.
Say, perhaps, his was never all the blame,
to keep the fetters and deny the art,
in seeking what he thought an honest name,
taking their wages to delude the heart.
The chisel used to square a common stone
might have made sculptured images as well,
to ease that aching bred into the bone.
Penitence burned him in denial's hell,
living his life in ways that were not meant;
in a vain purpose losing fair intent.

THE STROLLERS

They'll crash your door when evenings fall
to eat you out of house and hall,
said Finlay Mac an Aba.

A ranting, roving idle crew
who'll pay you but a song or two,
said Finlay Mac an Aba.

I'll not attempt their pedigree
nor tell their doubtful history,
said Finlay Mac an Aba.

With dogs at heel, a hungry horde
who plunder folk of bed and board,
said Finlay Mac an Aba.

But mind, for all their ruffian state,
the songs they sing are worth their meat,
said Finlay Mac an Aba.

So see you write down all their rhymes
and mine as well, for sadder times,
said Finlay Mac an Aba.

OPEN DAY: STATELY HOME

Far away over the edge of the wood
the gentle hills roll skyward.
I walk in vacant and in pensive mood
across his lordship's greensward.

In this country my line is just as long,
though from a clod-breaking strain,
not even, as some covet, from the wrong
blanket side of distaff line.

Good of him, letting me walk for a pound
all over his policies,
gazing, like one of his real peers, around
these gentrified solaces.

I thrust away my envy of his hall,
my coin clinking in *his* sack;
my growl that every ashlar in his wall
lies upon a miner's back.

Just for today I am Rouget de Lisle,
hearing a far beat of drums,
till peasant blood and bones recall the real:
in the end no tumbril comes.

WHEN I WAS YOUNG

from the Gaelic of Mairi Mhór nan Óran (Mary MacPherson),
1821–1898

Easement of sadness in early rising
on a May morning and I in Os,
one to another the cattle calling,
the dawn arising above the Storr;
a spear of sunlight upon the mountains
saw the last shadow of darkness gone,
the blithesome lark high above me singing
brought back to mind days when I was young.

A memory mingled with joy and sadness;
I lack the words that can tell them true,
each case and change of my mind and body
far from the glen whose bright peace I knew;
the river rippling so gently seawards,
my own speech echoed in the streamlet's flow,
sweet sang the mavis in budding branches
to wake the memories of long ago.

In careless joy I would roam the moorland,
the heather tips brushing on my dress,
through mossy knowes without help of footgear
when ice was forming on the lochan's face.
Seeking the sheep on the mountain ridges,
light as the snipe over meadow grass,
each mound and lochan and rolling hollow . . .
these are the memories of time that's past.

I bring to mind all the things I did there
that will not fade till my story's end;
walking in winter to prayer or wedding,
my only lantern a peat in hand;
the splendid youngsters, with song and dancing . . .
gone are their days now and sad the glen;
now Andrew's croft under shrouding nettles
brings back to mind how our days were then.

How I would travel each glen and hill-top,
herding the cattle with tranquil mind,
with lively youngsters now long in exile,
a sturdy breed without foolish pride.
Pasture and ploughland now heath and rushes,
where sickle swept and the sheaf was tied.
Could I see dwellings again and people
as once in youth, there I'd gladly bide.

There I would climb on the mountain shoulder
to take my ease on the grassy height,
my thought would leap in a blaze of wonder,
such beauty lying below my sight:
the royal thistle and the yellow primrose,
the golden blossom of sweet Saint Bride;
each joyous leaf under dew at evening
brings back a memory of youth's delight.

I turned my back on that fragrant homeland
to take the vessel that needs no breeze,
but sounds a horn to put power in motion
and set her course from the island seas.

My heart was crushed and the tears were flowing,
going to a place lacking song or peace,
where there's no thistle or nodding gowan,
rush bank or heather or grassy lease.

RIMBAUD, LATER PERIOD

Tonight I take my last walk in the glen,
beside the waters I have known so well;
I doubt if they will flow for me again,
in those dry places where men buy and sell.

No more of lines forged out of agony,
now mother-wit frees me from foolishness,
living at last as prudence counsels me,
to vend my thoughts in profitable dress.

I shun the need for trees and sky and water,
the stabbing dream that left me no defence;
tight office roofs will shelter me the better,
where sober speech supplies a richer chance.

UNREGENERATE

Holyman came to call me to those old ways
that I won free of after many a year,
having lost all faith now in the way he prays,
demanding help for favour of love, or fear.

Last night again I almost worshipped the moon,
standing so full and fair above the clouds,
but men will build cathedrals up there soon,
say new selenic prayers to dodge their shrouds.

Missing the point. The moon's worth looking at
just for that still moment that is forever.
The earth is beautiful whether it's round or flat,
Holyman's prayers have grown too long, too clever.

Familiar of ferret, net-plier,
foul-hooker on the waterside,
walks under the stars of a cool night.

Torch light on oak branch,
the silence smashed;
bird in the pocket and run.

Along the backs of hedges,
familiar ditches,
thrill of the chase and the prey.

A forkful of fowl stops
between plate and mouth in the high hall;
at the wrong end of the land a keeper curses
the thieving shot that echoes in the night.

Above the hall, the hunter, the hunted,
Orion stalks the hours to the verge of dawn.

DROVE ROAD

A thousand years of hooves beat this old way,
through the long glens below the dangerous hills
where eyes in ambush envied beef and fells,
hoping with whetted steel to hold at bay
the tough lean kerns. There's few would win the day
against these stubborn drovers. For slim gain,
father, son, brothers, plaided to wind and rain,
mingled their sweat and blood with the road's clay.

Down to the machair through the scattered craigs,
wading cold water, sliding over scree
towards the market pens and chaffering words.

Then back through hazard over the moss-hags,
bearing home simple goods, their modest fee.
We curse the road-bends where they walked their herds.

THREAVE TOWER

The other day again I left the car,
went over damp flat holms to the wide river
where the old keep stands square upon its ait,
splitting the waters for a sure defence
till powder baffled steel and the wall fell.

A startled hare rose up before my feet;
a pheasant lumbered up into the mist;
a moorhen fleet upon the still water.
There was no other there but the mailed ghosts
along the line of gaping embrasures.

They inched the great gun on the hill's vantage,
to pierce the ten-foot wall. An old tale says:
my lord, so sure no shot could breach the stone,
calmly enjoyed his meal in the wide room
till a flying shard cut off his lady's hand.

Old fanciful stories: mortar mixed with blood,
the men hanged for example above the gate,
the privilege of castle, slavery of cot-house,
grand silks over monster bodies, the coarse peasantry,
the feuds of envy, greed, malicious pride.

Eyes looked at me through time from lancet windows;
across long centuries their harness jingled.
I walked away from grey imaginings
till safely out of bowshot, hearing the sentry's voice:
What better now, in your own squalid day?

FAMILIARITY BREEDS CONTEMPT

Now television has allowed the proles
to have a good look at the Eminent,
we sans-culottes may scan with more intent,
noses for wens and skins for blackhead-holes,
discovering that they too have scars and moles
just like the more plebeian element.
Such epidermal flaws on dame and gent
liken the Mob to those with Higher Goals.

Now we're *all* privileged to see a lord
waggling his eyebrows, sucking his moustache.
But still, they're winning till they start to speak
and none of them has said a single word
worth listening to. What earns them all that *cash*?
Why didn't The Revolution start last week?

BUG UNIVERSE

The salmonella bug in the minestrone
looked up into its firmament and saw
a myriad vegetables stretching to infinity.
Phenomena, it knew, born of sheer chance –
absurd to think some fairy-tale Cook had sliced
that wondrous carrot-Mars, onion-ring-Saturn,
asteroid-peas, the noodle-comet-tails.
It knew beyond any possible shadow of doubt
that a soupy medium filled up all that space.
Absurd to think of the myth its pals believed,
that some day would come a marvellous transmigration
to a warm and heavenly gut beyond the pot.

SEPTEMBER DRY SPELL

The autumn walks are best, just at the start
when the high trees still wave their summer dress,
and the first hips, rowans, blackberries
whisper their coloured message of mortality
that quiet strollers hear above the cars,
roaring from nowhere on to god-knows-where.

Spires in the distance dream over sunlit naves,
locked against weekday vandals until prayers
bring in the pious, or the public figure
nursing his image in the lap of the gods.
The Sunday chariots scour the countryside,
carrying bored offspring eager to be home,
bearing their load of pre-arthritic bones.

Where have they all gone, the progenitors
who passed the baton down the vanished years?
Sorted as sheep or goats in their final pens?
Mere fertiliser to the graveyard grass?

On the high road between baptism and scepticism,
between wisdom and awareness of ignorance,
the clouds of glory shrivel to tattered wrack.

The holymen flourish their whips and scorpions,
the fundamentalists ride upon flaming tridents.
The cars speed past over the flattened fauna,
till the spear is sundered
and the chariots burn in the fire.

GREYNESS

In this quiet place of hills and trees and water,
best sometimes are the grey days when fine mist
is cool against the face, when suddenly
out of the dying afternoon, shapes loom
into the vision.

Best still when there is no other
to break the silence with talk,
no other foot to walk upon this summit.
Only the sheep and the black cattle here
to move upon the sight, breathe living air.

When the eye is robbed
of its vista of distant hills,
when the foot stops and the ear
listens into the stillness.

The mind to be held firm
against encroaching images,
of those old ghosts that move upon the moor
defying a pragmatic nothingness.

SEAL WOMEN

Remember in the taking of seal women
how such wild beauties were constrained to stay:
their cast hides seized by mortals, stowed away,
although their briny souls denied them heaven.

Being in the end the merest magical beasts,
despite silk skin, soft eyes and flowing hair.
Yet their desertion left an aching there,
when seas won back from men their secret breasts.

SUNDAY DRAGONFLIES

This is the day our fathers set apart
for mankind's homage and for quiet rest:
these demoiselles flit out their lives unblest;
the credit's given to a mindless art.
As heretic and pagan as the next,
I share with dragonflies the reeds and lake,
growing and flowing here for their own sake,
by no pale far Platonic shadow fixed.
The sounds that sing here are not made by man:
wind among sedge, call of a thousand birds
oblivious of any maker's plan
or echoing spell of legendary words.
Yet these long flies that dance from blade to blade . . .
by what dark hazard were such jewels made?

THE EXILED MANDARIN

After the many years,
hiding away beyond the far frontier,
I sought in distance for the quiet mind;
now waking dreams return to plague me here,
of those thronged corridors I left behind.

Had I not many cares?
All cruel ambition, enmity was there.
For all that, of my fortune I repined,
now the branch trembles and the leaf turns sere,
a sharp scent comes upon the southern wind.

DAMP THOUGHTS FROM A COUNTRY CHARGE, 1859

on first peeping into Darwin's 'Origin of Species'

Under the gable the dark waters rise;
the rain it raineth every single day,
tears, idle tears still gather to the eyes,
no solace now to drive the glooms away.
The foul Darwinian pack of cunning lies
rings in the head each time one tries to pray.
To distant Vectis the dear queen has gone,
looking to Mr Tennyson, with blinds drawn.

Ravenous nature, red in tooth and claw,
breeds beasts that gnaw each other in the night . . .
into their dens and holts they cruelly draw
those smaller fry on which they can alight,
to crunch them whole in an unfeeling maw,
as hedgehogs chumble beetles, awful sight . . .
or cooks plunge lobsters in the boiling pot . . .
(but we have special rights there, have we not?).

Unsolaced by his baccy or his port,
our great Lord Alfred loses inspiration . . .
poor clergymen have now become the sport
of all the gutter scribblers in the nation.
Impudent chaps of the mechanic sort
attack our works with ratiocination;
neither strong drink nor the pure-water wagon
delay dark visions of the primal dragon.

Perhaps the water climbing from the ditches
to cloak the surface of this dreary fen
is like old Noah's warning, meant to switch us,
back to those Comfortable Words again
that keep the church in cassocks, coats and breeches,
and win a diocese for Oxford men,
help us to love a Lord, and love your Graces,
who keep the ignoble plebs in their right places.

Here in our knuckle-end, the Northern Fastness,
a snuff of the Metropolis arrives:
exotic southern needs and new *Brief Lives*.
A window on the life style of our masters,
the Ascot fashions, the career disasters.
We drink their exploits with our heathen eyes
as they drink up the champagne that supplies
such wit as thrives upon their lusher pastures.

They tell us that our land is Much Improved.
Old Useless Industry now cleared away,
ironmasters gone, who made our lives so hard.

There's leisure now the steel mill's been removed
to read about their booming, brighter day,
free gifts of Nuclear Waste for our back yard.

pages 2, 22, 79	'Knowe': Scots form of knoll (small rounded hill).
pages 16, 85	'Machair': flat grassland on foreshore (Gaelic).
page 29	It is said that descendants of the family of the MacVurich (Gaelic MacMhuirich) poets – tailors no longer able to read Gaelic – cut up vellum manuscripts, ignorant of their poetic value.
pages 49, 85	'Moss-hag': a boghole on a peaty moor.
page 64	The poem's title is translated from Catullus, '*Nam risu inepto res ineptior nullast*', 39.16.
page 66	'Fergus': leader of the invading Scoti from Ireland in the sixth century.
	'Tattie Blight': the potato famine of the nineteenth century.
	'Kentigern's salmon': refers to Glasgow's coat of arms.
	'Dear Green Place': a translation of Glaschu, the Gaelic for Glasgow.
page 77	Finlay Mac an Aba (MacNab) was a sixteenth-century Gaelic poet.
page 81	'Lease': an open pasture or common.